SOUTHWESTERN STUDIES

MONOGRAPH NO. 45

Considerations on the Politica
and Social Situation of

The Mexican Republic 1847

translated and edited by

DENNIS E. BERGE

TEXAS WESTERN PRESS
THE UNIVERSITY OF TEXAS AT EL PASO

ISBN 0-87404-103-1

$3 PER COPY

ABOUT THE AUTHOR

Dennis Berge is a native of Minnesota and a long time resident of California. He received his undergraduate education and an M.A. in history at San Diego State University, pursued his doctoral studies at the University of California at Berkeley in the history of the American West, and received his Ph.D. in 1965. Since 1963 he has been a member of the history faculty at San Diego State University. From 1971 to 1974 he was chairman of the history department.

Considerations on the Political and Social Situation of

THE MEXICAN REPUBLIC 1847

Translated and edited by DENNIS E. BERGE

IN APRIL, 1847, a disconsolate Mexican politician named José Fernando Ramírez recorded a gloomy commentary on the tumultuous events of the preceding months as he worked on his personal correspondence. Military actions in the war against the United States had gone badly. To the north the battle of Angostura had brought destruction to the best troops Mexico could put in the field, and to the south a new invasion through the port of Veracruz posed an even greater threat. Moreover, a barracks revolution in the capital by dissident National Guard battalions had thrown the entire Mexican war effort into chaos, and forced a drastic shake-up of the federal government. Ramírez was appalled by the revolution, which so clearly jeopardized Mexico's future. "I tell you with a heavy heart," he wrote, "that everyone, everyone without exception, behaved in such a manner that we richly deserve the scorn and derision of all cultivated peoples. We are nothing, absolutely nothing."[1]

The despair that seized Ramírez at that moment was shared by many Mexicans during the war with the United States, for the war was an exceedingly frustrating affair. Mexico's cause seemed so clearly in the right that to lose the struggle would be an injustice, yet one defeat followed another in the apparently inexorable advance of the Americans. The small size of the invading armies only aggravated the feeling of frustration among Mexicans, and as military reverses mounted a wave of introspection, self-analysis, and sometimes self-condemnation emerged from both political and intellectual circles. Partisan alliances and the general mood of despair influenced the public dialogue that followed, but the result was nevertheless an exchange of views that gives remarkable insight into the forces buffeting a very troubled nation in the midst of a war that she did not want, and by any reasonable estimate, could not win.

The Original Document

The treatise which appears on the following pages was published originally in Mexico in 1848 by the printing house of Valdes y Redondes with the title *Consideraciones sobre la situación política y social de la república mexicana, en el año 1847*. As a political document it has created considerable interest among historians concerned with the development of liberal ideology in Mexican political thought.[2] It has received less attention for its analysis of Mexico's internal problems as they affected the conduct of the war, even though it was this relationship that was responsible for its publication. Bitter in tone, filled with pessimism, and partisan in approach, the essay nevertheless lays bare the divisions which tore at Mexican society, and which seemed only to worsen as the war went on.

In December, 1847, which is when the essay was dated, the war was in its final phases. The capital had fallen to Winfield Scott's invading army three months before, and many of Mexico's other major cities — including Veracruz, Puebla, Tampico, Monterrey, and Saltillo — were occupied by the Americans. Santa Anna had resigned the presidency, and the remnants of the Mexican army, which had collapsed following the loss of Mexico City, were scattered throughout central Mexico. A provisional government under the control of the *moderados* operated from Querétaro, and was in the process of negotiating an end to the war with the American diplomat Nicholas Trist, but faced considerable opposition from Mexicans who wished to continue the fight. It was an hour of trial, and the difficulty of Mexico's position is reflected in the document which follows.

There has been, and remains, some uncertainty over the authorship of this pamphlet. It was undeniably the product of one or more politically liberal figures, but it was signed only by "Varios Mexicanos," which raises the question as to whether more than one author actually was involved. The slightly different format in the two major divisions of the essay is one piece of evidence arguing for multiple authorship, as is a pattern of redundancy between the two parts on such subjects as the role of the clergy, the evils of civil and military appointments, and the low status of trade labor. There is a general consistency of views throughout the essay, except that the lower orders of clergy are in some places treated more harshly than in others, and the focus of the piece begins to shift from independent Mexico to the subject of Spanish colonial heritage with the discussion of crafts and trade, which comes near the end of Part One. Once begun, the indictment of Spanish institutions and customs continues to mount throughout the second part of the essay, culminating in a ringing denunciation of Spain's legacy to the New World.

For present purposes the identification of individual authorship is perhaps not as important as a recognition of the political ideology reflected in the pamphlet. The doctrines of Mexican liberalism had taken shape over a period of two decades through the writings of men such as José María Luis Mora, Lorenzo de Zavala, José Bernardo Couto, and Mariano Otero, so that a general set of ideas had been put together that served as a basis for the liberal movement. As the label suggests, the objective of this movement was the reformation of Mexican society. Decentralized government and rule through republican institutions stood among its first principles, as did a concern for the worth and welfare of the individual citizen. Liberals consequently endorsed such concepts as freedom of press and speech, equality before the law, and an open pattern of economic opportunity, and they were critical of corporate entities that enjoyed privileged positions in Mexican society. The Church and the army were thus their favorite targets, while the civil service, large landowners, and industrial and commercial interests operating under government favoritism also came under attack. Because liberals were in conflict with different aspects of the status quo they tended to make unfavorable reflections upon the origins of existing institutions and customs, which in many cases were products of the Spanish colonial system. Their attitude toward Mexico's Spanish heritage was heavily conditioned by this factor, though the hostility in this essay is unusually sharp.

Perhaps no spokesman was as important to the growth of liberal thought as José María Luis Mora, a forceful essayist and journalist exiled from Mexico in 1834, and a resident of France and England from then until his death in 1850. During the war years Mora was thus isolated from the intellectual ferment developing within Mexican society, but in his absence a number of other writers – including Luis de la Rosa, José Bernardo Couto, Melchor Ocampo, Guillermo Prieto, Mariano Otero, and Juan Bautista Morales – came into their own in articulating the views of liberal reformers. The present pamphlet is a notable example of their contributions during this period, and it illustrates a process through which they brought the doctrinal differences between Mexican liberals and conservatives into new and bold relief. In the years following the war this was to lead to a heightened sense of political awareness in Mexico, which in turn was a presage to the era of The Reform.

Author Identification: Otero

One of the persons identified with the authorship of this pamphlet is Mariano Otero, a young *moderado* politician who had established a reputation as a political theorist prior to the war.[3] In 1842 Otero published an important treatise called *Ensayo sobre el verdadero estado de la cuestión social y política que se agita en la república mexicana* which contained similarities in approach and analytical method to the pamphlet presented here, and this has led some scholars to believe that he was at least partially responsible for its publication.[4] The similarities are undeniably strong enough to lend weight to this conclusion, but the acceptance of Otero as sole author also raises some questions. If he wrote it by himself it seems doubtful that he would have published it anonymously, for Otero had demonstrated in several instances that he welcomed the role of provacateur, and he did not shrink from notoriety. As one of several authors, however, he could have been pressured by more cautious colleagues into an agreement to remain anonymous. The general tone of the commentary was enough to insure hostility from the conservative element of Mexican society, but it was in the final few pages that the pamphlet invited even more serious condemnation. To even suggest the acceptance of a United States protectorate over Mexico was, under the circumstances, an act bordering on treason. This might cause many to shrink from an admission of authorship, but in the case of Otero it raises a question of another sort. In September, 1847, Otero broke with fellow *moderados* to denounce the abortive peace negotiations conducted with Nicholas Trist during the preceding weeks, arguing that the Mexican peace commissioners proposed to dishonor their country by surrendering territory that had not been contested when the war began.[5] The American occupation of Mexico City came shortly after this incident, and Otero was soon thrown into prison by American military authorities for public denunciation of the United States occupation forces.[6] Released through the intercession of the First Alcalde of the Mexico City municipal government, he made his way to Querétaro, the temporary seat of government. Here he opposed ratification of the Treaty of Guadalupe Hidalgo, and, this failing, entered into the post-war government as Secretary of Foreign Affairs. Otero then brought formal charges of treason against Francisco Suarez Iriarte, the First Alcalde who had arranged for his release from prison only months before. The basis of the accusation was Otero's assertion that Suarez Iriarte had collaborated with the enemy during the occupation and had conspired for the permanent occupation or annexation of Mexico by the United States. The charges were heard by the Chamber of Deputies due to Suarez Iriarte's own standing as a Deputy, and it decided by a vote of 48 to 27 that he should stand trial in a criminal court. The untimely death of Suarez Iriarte, however, brought an end to the proceedings at this point.[7]

The purpose in describing this facet of Otero's conduct during the war is that it reveals a militancy not consistent with the benign attitude shown in this pamphlet toward the occupation army, and toward the prospect of an American protectorate over Mexico. The interesting possibility exists that Otero held these views privately, but if he did he concealed his secret. After brief service as Secretary of Foreign Affairs he retired from public life in mid-1848, apparently because he was depressed by Mexico's experiences. In 1850 a cholera epidemic swept Mexico City and claimed Otero as one of its victims. He was thirty-three years old at the time of his death.[8]

Other Possibilities: Morales

The uncertainties surrounding Otero's authorship raise the question of whether there was any other writer who may have been more likely to have produced the essay. There were many among both *moderado* and *puro* circles who are eligible in terms of general political philosophy, but the candidacy of Juan Bautista Morales deserves special consideration. Morales was, like Otero, a *moderado,* and a political essayist of considerable standing. Born in 1788, he held a variety of political and judicial offices between 1824 and 1842, when he joined the staff of the newspaper *El siglo diez y nueve* as a political columnist. He proved to be a skillful spokesman for the *moderado* cause, and he developed a flair for satire and parody that brought his services into demand by a number of other newspapers in the years that followed.[9] The most successful of Morales' journalistic activities was the writing of a parody on both the Socratic method and the foibles of Mexican society which he called *El gallo pitagórico,* and which *El siglo diez y nueve* serialized in 1842. It was in December of this year also that Morales was thrown into prison for criticizing the policy of Texan reconquest preached by the Santa Anna government. He was released after a short confinement, but he had become identified with the group of *moderados* that opposed war over the question of Texas. In the spring of 1848 he was appointed special consultant to the Ministry of Foreign Affairs by Acting President José Joaquín Herrera, who was then attempting to garner support for ratification of the Treaty of Guadalupe Hidalgo. Morales himself believed that peace was necessary if Mexico wished to save her nationality, and he founded a newspaper he called *Los Debates* to popularize this point of view.[10]

In his general political views Morales was anti-militarist, anti-centralist, and anti-privilege; he was also a believing Catholic who was extremely critical of the Mexican priesthood. These were views so generally held by Mexican liberals that they do not set Morales apart, nor are they particularly helpful in determining if he may have written the pamphlet. It contains other similarities to his known works, however, that may be of more importance. His general tone of conciliation toward the Americans is in marked contrast to the militancy shown by Otero, and it harmonizes more easily with the point of view developed in the pages that follow. The satire injected into the narrative is also reminiscent of the Morales touch, and the commentary upon trade prohibitions and the role of foreign entrepreneurs in Mexican commerce is similar to that developed by Morales in *El gallo pitagórico*.[11] There are also two themes developed in the essay that perhaps may be regarded as idiocyncratic, and that also appear in the writings of Morales. One is a special concern for military casualties and the plight of their families; the other is the argument that governmental income and expenditures in Mexico were determined in the wrong order, thus raising the question of the extent to which one activity was by its nature a function of the other.

The best that can be said in light of the above is that the essay's author remains a matter of some uncertainty, but that among the logical candidates are Mariano Otero and Juan Bautista Morales. Like Otero, Morales made no known claim of ownership in later life, although he remained on the scene for several years longer than the young *moderado*. His last public office was that of President of the Supreme Court of Justice, which he received in 1855 and held until his death in July, 1856.

Introduction to the Document

A foreign army of from ten to twelve thousand men has penetrated from Veracruz to the capital of the republic. With the exception of its coastal bombardment, the battle at Cerro Gordo, and the minor engagements it has had with Mexican troops near the capital itself, it has found virtually no enemies to fight in its long march across three of the most important and heavily populated states of the Mexican federation, containing more than two million inhabitants. This is a development of such significance that it cannot help but give rise to the most serious reflections.

Men with little insight judge issues by looking at events instead of causes, and usually come to the wrong conclusions. It is consequently not surprising to have seen the Mexican people referred to in some foreign newspapers as an effeminate people, and as a degenerate race that does not know how to govern or defend itself. But rational men are not satisfied only to look at surface events, and try to discover their underlying causes. Such men will easily find in Mexico what is actually responsible for our people remaining as indifferent spectators to the present contest, instead of taking an active part in the struggle. Once these reasons have been uncovered only the blindest partiality could lead a person to claim that what are inevitable results of specific and determined causes could be special defects of the Mexican race.

What we propose to do in this publication is to describe as clearly as possible the many and heterogeneous elements that compose the society of the Mexican republic, as this is undoubtedly the best way to show the actual reasons for its present decay and misfortunes. We hope thus to correct errors coming from the lips of even the most reputable persons; errors which interpret defects common to the human species as pecularities of the Mexican race.

In misfortune nations, like individuals, fall victim to every manner of slander and insult. The ignorance and malevolence common to people who indulge in universal criticism allow them to engage in slander which makes the situation of an unfortunate even more painful and miserable, but they never justify or exculpate him. This has been the fortune of all peoples — of men in general — since the beginning of time, and Mexico certainly has no reason to be excepted. She has taken her turn now, and she can endure her fortunes without dismay, content in the knowledge that the same people who are insulting her today have more than once suffered equal or greater humiliations.

But if it is true that the mob is generally callous and unsympathetic toward one who suffers misfortune, it is also true that some men are exceptions. They are determined to form their own opinions from the results of analysis and impartial deliberation, and they attempt to be just. They do not consider the presently agonized Mexican republic to be a nation suffering from defects that originate in racial emasculation or degeneration, but as a nation that has fallen victim to its vicious education, and to faulty organization. With this in mind we believe that Mexico deserves far better from other nations than their scorn and derision. If it cannot yet hope for assistance from the other nations of the world in the name of simple justice at least it can hope for the sympathies that every decent person feels for the one who sustains a just cause and succumbs after great sacrifice, not to the greater strength of the enemy, but because of the inaction that results when a society is divided by opposing and incompatible interests.

We will not indulge in useless polemics, partly because we dislike them, and partly because it seems clear that there is no need to make arguments to vindicate the Mexican republic when a simple description of its internal alignments ought to be explanation enough for its conduct in the present situation.

In order to accomplish the purpose of this publication clearly we have divided it into two parts. In the first, we will deal with the population in general, and in particular with the producing classes. In the second we will discuss the privileged classes.

FIRST PART

I *Population*

Our data on the population of the republic is very inexact, for some give it but little more than six million inhabitants while others estimate it at more than nine. We place the figure near seven million. Of this, according to the most reliable information, four million are Indian and three of the European race, mixed largely with Indian.[12]

II *Indians*

The Indians are found scattered throughout the republic, gathered in small communities and actually forming a family apart from the white and mixed races.[13] Their present wretched way of life is little or no different from that of the subjects of the emperor Moctezuma. The only difference between then and now is in the elimination of idolatry with its barbarous human sacrifices, for present day Indians have learned in their fashion to worship God and His saints, and to hope for happiness in the next life. This is something one might expect them to depend upon strongly, for they are thoroughly convinced that they have nothing good to hope for in this vale of tears. Neither during the time of the Viceroyalty nor after independence has an effective system of education been adopted for members of this race that would help them to improve their own fortunes, take them from the brutish conditions in which they live, nor make them useful to society. Neither then nor now have they been taught anything but to fear God, the priest, and the *alcalde*. The ignorance in which they live is so complete that it is safe to say that perhaps three-fourths of them have not even heard about our independence. It is even more believable that they could live with such misconceptions when you realize that in many places tribute for the crown is still collected, in the same way and for the same object that donations are requested for the ransom of prisoners and for the holy places of Jerusalem.

The occupation to which they are usually fated calls for them to work the land for a small wage, and as this is usually not enough to cover the costs of their dismal existence they frequently ask the owner of the hacienda they serve for an advance on their wages. This obliges them to remain there until they pay off the indebtedness. For this reason, and because the wages they earn are scarcely enough to live on, it is inevitable that the moment an Indian makes such a loan the hacienda owner loses the sum he loans and the Indian sells himself to the master of the hacienda and becomes his property. The result is that although Indian slavery is a specific violation of law it exists in fact in many parts of the republic.

Another factor is that through the system that governs the Church in Mexico the so-called high clergy of the capital and other bishoprics live in opulence, but the village priests have no other way to subsist than from parochial fees. We consequently find these representatives of the God of goodness and mercy obliged to permit no Indian to be born, to marry, or to die without penalty, or without paying the "established" fees, and this is the way they collect the small income upon which they depend for their subsistence.

The Indians that live around the great population centers go there to sell their vegetables, poultry, wood, charcoal and other humble products, and their small profits are taken from them at the city gates by tax collectors, who commit the most infamous and repugnant extortions in the name of the nation.

To give the final stroke to this faithful picture of the sorrowful existence of the Indians we need merely add that the only active part they take in the public affairs of the country is to serve as soldiers in the army, and they are obliged to do this by force. While they are in this service they do not really serve the nation, but only act as instruments for the aggrandizement of their commanders. In peacetime they are given little to eat and plenty of punishment, and in war they are frequently abandoned at the moment of danger. It is easy to understand how this important part of the nation's population could show a complete lack of interest in the preservation of a social order which makes them its victims. The Indians have undeniably seen the coming of the North American army with the same indifference with which they formerly saw the coming of the Spanish armies when they conquered the country, and with the same passiveness with which they saw our troops come and go in our continual internal revolutions following independence. Without other needs than those which the semi-savage state in which they live demands, neither bound to nor benefitting from society in any way, with no share in the interests or affections of their countrymen, and confident that their abject condition could not become worse, they view everything that can possibly happen to them with the utmost indifference.

III White and Mixed Race

We pass now to an examination of the three million inhabitants of European and mixed race which make up the capital and other cities and important towns in the republic. Of the total number we can safely conclude that some 1,800,000 souls are women, children and old people, leaving to us some 1,200,000 useful men or, more accurately, potentially useful, because in reality they are not, as we will show as we go along.

There is first the matter of 300,000 men, which is the total of the number employed in agriculture, textile manufacturing, mining, commerce, and some arts and trades. The remaining 900,000 consist of unproductive classes, such as the clergy, with all its dependents and hangers-on, the military, civil servants, lawyers, doctors, and finally, the multitude of idlers and vagabonds that abound in the principal cities of the republic.

Through this frank description the uneviable position of the one-fourth of the male poplation which labors and produces, and upon which the other three-fourths necessarily live, can be seen. There is an acute imbalance here, which is the origin of the impoverishment and stagnation of all the sources of public wealth, and sufficient cause not only to destroy the nascent Mexican republic, but to undermine the most flourishing nation on earth.

IV Commerce

Import activities, with very few exceptions, are found in the hands of foreigners. Thanks to the hostility and intolerance that come inevitably from the monastic education we inherit from our good fathers these foreigners neither could nor do respond with any interest to the fortunes of a country in which they are dedicated only to doing business, and as soon as they make enough money to satisfy their desires they go to enjoy it somewhere else. The import trade amounts to some sixteen million pesos annually, and there is no hope that it will increase while we do not have more people to consume European goods, and while we do not have other goods to exchange in return. As long as Mexico has nothing to export except money the importation of merchandise will always be approximately equal to the value of silver we are able to mine.[14]

In addition to these natural disadvantages the revenue system that has prevailed until now does as much or more to prevent a healthy foreign trade. The basic policy of this system has been to impose high tariffs on all goods, hoping to thus increase revenues, to support an immense and costly customs service, and to further whatever measures greed and craftiness suggest in the formation of custom regulations.[15] Countless requirements have been placed upon the importer for both the landing of merchandise in ports and its shipment into the interior, and he is threatened with the loss of his merchandise for the slightest infringement of these regulations. The result of such a system has been what one might expect. Custom revenues have become progressively smaller, merchants in bad faith have consistently flouted the law by purchasing the compliance of public servants, and immorality has increased daily. It is impossible to correct the situation while the savings from evading increased taxes allow merchants to offer bribes of such magnitude that few men have the honor to refuse them. Finally, the many restrictions dreamed up to prohibit fraud have seemed only to antagonize and prejudice merchants and traders of good faith, causing endless difficulties.

For these reasons it should not seem strange that this branch of trade, which is so important to the prosperity of nations, is found languishing. Some merchants and other leading men have protested in vain against our tariff system, demonstrating how senseless and mischievous it is not only for commerce, but for the widely recognized interests of the national treasury. They have called in vain for the end of internal tariffs, demonstrating that they are a great obstacle to the mercantile trade and the origin of a thousand abuses and infamies. The miserable revenues they bring in could be replaced by almost any kind of direct tax, which could undoubtedly be collected more simply and economically. To these critics the customary response has been given that it is not yet time; that this will have to come later; and that for now innovations in this country are very dangerous. The men reputed to be our great economists, without whose opinion nothing is done in this field, are, in addition, civil servants. They are consequently very closely tied to the existing system, and oppose any change. Thoughtful men who ask for free and untaxed commerce are said to be visionaries, and merchants are regarded as suspicious characters whose design should never be trusted. This is because most government employees still think of merchants in the same way that Jews were regarded in the Middle Ages.

Retail trade – including both imports and domestic goods – is, with few exceptions, in the hands of Mexicans. Because this branch of commerce is dependent upon wholesale trade, however, it is also in a depressed state. Of all the Mexicans who follow this occupation only a few have modest success, while failures occur frequently. Most keep going only through severe economies, and even privations.

V *Agriculture*

We might begin our discussion of agriculture in Mexico by noting that three-fourths of the republic's territory is the property of various religious corporations.[16] Consequently, three-fourths of the so-called hacienda proprietors are proprietors in name only. In reality they are simply rentors, sometimes because these haciendas are in absolute possession of the clergy, and sometimes because all or part of the value stems from some form of investment capital from which the clergy expects a return.[17]

These circumstances help explain the general state of neglect of our farm lands, for there is no incentive for a man to improve property that is not his, and from which he only hopes to take as much as possible during the period of his lease. There is no reason for members of the clergy to improve the land either, as they are profit-takers rather than proprietors.

The general fortunes of the peasants are harder than one can imagine, inasmuch as they know not whether to fear a very bad or a very good year the most. In the former case it is obvious that they lose all or most of the harvest, but in the latter case the results are more or less the same. If the harvest is good there is a great surplus of farm products, and as the consumers neither increase nor could increase because of our scarcity of population the drop in prices is considerable. In this case the peasants who do not have enough capital to wait for a better time to sell their products profitably — and this includes the majority — are obliged to dump them, perhaps losing part of their capital, or at least the profits they hoped for during their year of labor and fatigue. If the peasant has enough capital he still gains no special benefit unless a good year is followed by two or three bad ones, for that is the only way he can sell the products he may have stored at higher prices. Consequently the peasant who possesses no other capital than that necessary to support the planting and cultivation of his fields each year has to smother the criminal wish that his neighbor's crops be destroyed, because this is the only way he can sell his own expeditiously and at a profit.

In view of these circumstances it is needless to point out that all the inventions and refinements made in other societies in recent years to improve agricultural operations or make them more economical have been of no help to the peasants of Mexico. In fact, it hardly seems necessary to refine this art in a country whose bountiful and almost untapped natural resources well reward the least efforts of man, and are easily capable of feeding fifteen or twenty times our present population. These factors make it evident that the depression of the agricultural class in Mexico is not due to a breakdown in the means of production, but to the lack of demand; and it is clear that while the population remains stationary there is no hope of prosperity for a segment of society that is first in importance to the real wealth and growth of a nation.

As we have noted, the consequences of our limited population put the peasant in the uneviable position of not being able to hope for decent profits except through the ruin of some of his companions. It is also a fact that even though these people are valuable to society, they, like merchants, are victims of our system of taxation. Because the tax rates established for the shipment of their products from one place to another are not made public, or are flouted, their fortunes often disappear into the greedy hands of treasury employees.

In addition to the many taxes that exist in Mexico for all working men, there is a matter of the tithe. It falls particularly hard upon the peasant, for it is exacted by the Church on the total value of his harvest. Although a law passed in 1833 makes this heavy contribution no longer obligatory many still pay it, sometimes because they consider it a matter of conscience and sometimes because they believe the sacrifice to be necessary in order to live in peace in a world of fanatics, and to avoid being treated as heretics. It is said that there have been several instances in which priests have refused to give dying peasants absolution for their sins unless they first arrange to turn over to the Church the equivalent of the tithes they had refused to pay because of the law mentioned above.

VI Administration of Justice

In addition to the other problems relating to commerce and agriculture a still greater mischief exists. It is a matter that could well destroy all society by undermining its foundations, and it particularly affects these two classes, which cannot exist or prosper except under the protection of order and public confidence.

This problem is the weakness in our administration of justice. Instead of a clear and precise legal code our laws are in chaos, to the point where the honest litigant joins the man of bad faith in choosing from a multitude of different laws that make the simplest case in the world an endless and contentious affair. Proceedings are so long and costly that whenever there is serious controversy you can predict that judicial proceedings will continue as long as the contending parties have the means and will to pay for them.

There are cases pending in Mexico that were first introduced more than a hundred years ago, and the action taken and money spent by successive generations have failed to bring the issues in question to a definite resolution.

The prisons, always filled with vicious and criminal men of all kinds living together indiscriminately, are anything but institutions of correction or punishment. It is more accurate to say that they are schools for prostitution and corruption. It is also a fact that the novice law breaker who enters them for the first time will leave them as a confirmed criminal, and will have lost all sense of shame. It is a rare thing to hear of the death of a criminal in the interest of justice, but crimes against property and even against life are repeated every day on the highways and in the cities. In the Mexico City prison alone there are usually 600, 800, or even 1000 criminals, and although most of them are not there for serious crimes there are many who have committed eight or more robberies or murders. These hardened criminals nevertheless spend months or years in their enclosures, and not a day passes but what they plot to escape and commit new crimes. This is natural in view of their freedom from punishment, and they succeed in mocking not only justice, but society itself.

It is important to point out here that no country can prosper when the fundamental basis of all organized societies, which is the guarantee of life and property, ceases to exist because of the abuse of a fair and orderly administration of justice. This is why Mexico can well call itself the land of accommodations. In order to avoid legal proceedings, which are always costly and never give satisfactory results, men find it necessary to deal with sharpsters, swindlers, forgers, and even with thieves and assassins. The adage that "a bad agreement is worth more than a good lawsuit" is the only code followed by prudent men, who hesitate to waste their time and money in suits and altercations that seem unpromising, for there is no certainty that they will be successful even if their claim is just. The merchant and landlord settle privately with debtors of bad faith and are forced to be satisfied with whatever they can get, knowing that if they go to court they will probably get nothing. The hacienda owner also placates the highwayman, lodging him in his own home and treating him as if he were his best friend, even though the man has robbed him several times. It would not occur to him to denounce the thief or surrender him to the authorities, for he knows that after serving a short time in prison he will be released to take his own revenge. Teamsters and traders, who are forced to live constantly on the highways due to their professions, are also obliged to cultivate friendly relations with the same thieves as the only means of insuring their own survival.

VII *Manufacturing*

The relative importance manufacturing now holds in Mexico is a recent development, dating from the first support it received from the government in 1830. This was the result of a misdirected attempt to increase our national wealth, or perhaps to flatter the vanity of ignorant men who believe that all we have to do to make our republic prosperous is to manufacture, so that we need buy nothing from foreigners. In order to halt the flow of money from the country the government ordered the creation of what is called the "Assistance Bank" with a capitalization of one million pesos to aid all who wished to establish any type of manufacturing.[18]

This "Assistance Bank" was, as they commonly say, a real Mount Parnassus, from which great sums were taken, always under the pretext of underwriting new industries. But rarely did any new production actually result from the use of these funds. With few exceptions the only activity the bank stimulated was in looking for pretexts to take as much money as possible, spending a small part of it on a few cylindrical looms to save appearances, and then leaving the government to be responsible for them – though God knows how.

Later, and as the only certain way to encourage manufacturing, the government prohibited the importation of cotton thread or fabrics into the republic, as well as other goods that could be manufactured in this country.[19] A number of factories were built in the shadow of this protection, for many were attracted by the exceptional returns made by those who had already become established, and believed that this was a promising venture.

Great fortunes were soon invested in these activities, and the manufacturing class, composed in large part of influential people, became an increasingly important part of our society. It vigorously supported trade restrictions as a matter of course, so that in 1840, when the government authorized textile shipments through the port of Matamoros in order to gain tariff revenue to support the Army of the North, these manufacturers objected violently. This was one of the principle reasons for which they started and supported a revolution that overthrew the administration the following year, resulting in a dictatorial government under the provisions of the notorious *Plan de Tacubaya.*[20] The government then gave industry considerable protection, extending import restrictions to many more items. Later on, in the departments, councils composed of the manufacturers were formed for the purpose of protecting their own interests. Their influence became so strong that in the Constitution of 1843 the general congress was forbidden "to repeal or suspend laws prohibiting the importation of goods prejudicial to native industry without the previous consent of two-thirds of the departmental assemblies."[21]

It seems incredible that the national legislature could be deprived of the power to legislate over a certain portion of society. This is in effect depriving society of its incontestable right to govern itself freely, and to reform or eliminate those things which are in some manner harmful. But nothing is impossible in Mexico, where private individuals and corporations, rather than the general interests of the country, have controlled the enactment of laws as a matter of course.

The gains from this industry have been what one might expect from an unnatural institution created against all the rules of reason and public convenience, and which cannot subsist save under the shadow of prohibitions and privilege. The public pays almost the same price for goods of domestic manufacture as for those that formerly came from abroad, and they are generally of worse quality. The national treasury has lost duties that would have brought in forty million pesos during the more than ten years of import prohibitions. The absence of these duties has been the source of the innumerable direct taxes that today weigh upon society, but they have never produced enough to fill the void left through the want of tariffs – partly because there has been neither method nor plan in the way in which they have been enacted, and partly because of the cost of their collection. The manufacturers have also failed to gain the great profits they were led to expect. A very few have become wealthy, but most have scraped along with a miserable return on the capital they have invested, and others have been ruined. The number of bankruptcies among those dedicated to this type of speculation has not been inconsiderable.[22]

According to the last "memorandum" published by the "General Congress of Industry" in 1845, the principal branch of industry, in addition to some manufacturers of paper, woolen cloth, window glass, and other products of less importance, is that of cotton yarn and cloth, as there are 128 plants of this type established in the republic today. Some of them have been located at points convenient for the masking of the clandestine introduction of foreign cotton cloth and yarn, which we have never lacked in this country in spite of the prohibitions. In view of the great profits available to the importers, this was only to be expected.

VIII Mines

In the midst of the confusion and depression at all levels of society the mining industry alone presents a bright picture, and one which gives indication of increasing prosperity. It symbolizes the fact that in this country everything in nature, with the exception of man himself, attempts to contribute to the well being and happiness of the people. The products of the mines of the republic in silver, and in gold coin and bullion, surpass eighteen million pesos, and this sum could be doubled, or even tripled, if quicksilver were not so expensive. Nevertheless, the profits from this industry go only to the owners of the mines and to the people engaged in their exploitation, and the rest of society gains nothing from these undertakings except through the greater circulation of money in the market place. This is always transitory and momentary, for each year we import just about the same amount that the mines produce in gold and silver. As we have noted elsewhere, these are the only products we have to offer in foreign exchange.

IX Crafts and Trades

As far as the portion of Mexicans dedicated to crafts and trades is concerned there is not much that can be said that is favorable. An unfortunate attitude inherited from the Spaniards still exists among us, for they were filled with ideas of chivalry and nobility, and taught us to despise every man dedicated to a trade. In order to be considered an honorable man it was necessary to be a soldier, a civil servant, a priest, a lawyer, or perhaps a doctor. All other classes were socially inferior, and even merchants were viewed with contempt, being referred to as rag pickers. As a result of these ideas, which were both ridiculous and pernicious, no heads of family of limited means wished — nor still wish — to educate their sons to a trade. They recoil at the thought of placing them as clerks in a commercial house, for besides the stupid prejudice they have toward any trade, they regard this as the equivalent of selling one's soul. To work in an office or warehouse seems to them to be denigrating.

These prejudices are so strong that even artisans who have worked at a decent and honorable trade do not pass it on to their sons, but instead send them to school to study law or medicine. If not this, they take them from school as soon as they know something of reading, writing, and arithmetic, and arrange with some person of influence to have the government grant them a position in the civil service or the military. This is not usually difficult to do, and when he does it the good artisan finds reason to be proud, and he is satisfied that his sons will be better off than he. There are also many fathers that formerly would have taught their sons a trade, but now prefer to give them none, and leave them instead to their own fortunes so that they can seek life as God gives them to understand it — but not, of course, as decent men. They will not dishonor themselves by working at a trade, for to this group of men all work is dishonorable. They do not believe it is dishonorable, however, to spend their lives as vagrants and swindlers.

It is because of this situation that the republic is plagued by hundreds of generals and thousands of officials and officers, civil servants, clerics, lawyers, and doctors, while it is impossible to find a single Mexican distinguished in any craft or trade. In every city of any importance the best architect, the best sculptor, the most gifted painter, the best cartmaker, the most intelligent tapestry maker, the most accomplished cabinet maker, the best gilder, the best blacksmith, the best tailor, and even the best shoemaker, are not Mexicans, but foreigners. What makes this so tragic is that Mexicans do not lack talent, and they are famous for their adaptive ability. In consequence, however, artisans that form the most important part of the population of more fortunate countries because of their intelligence and energy are ineffective and despised in Mexico, partly because they are so few in number, and partly because of the ignorance and disrepute in which they live.

X *General Observations*

This has been an honest and straightforward account of the conditions in which the productive classes that comprise such a small part of the Mexican population live, and it explains the source of their permanent misery. It also explains the selfishness and indifference with which these people have generally viewed the war the republic presently endures. Whatever else might be said, the fine and generous sense of patriotism that leads people in other countries to prefer a thousand deaths to the acceptance of the slightest offense against their country cannot exist among an uneducated people who have been torn by thirty-six years of hardship and misery.

The eleven years that encompassed the war of independence were years of bloodshed, devastation, and ruin for the productive classes of the country, and it is no exaggeration to state that the losses suffered by these classes during that long war amounted to hundreds of millions of pesos. When independence came, landowners, farmers, merchants, and others who wanted order as a prelude to prosperity and a promising future told themselves that a new era was about to begin that would make up for the years of hardship they had endured, but they were mistaken. In the twenty-six years that have passed since independence we have attempted several forms of government, but these attempts have in reality been superficial. Because we have never undertaken the meaningful reforms demanded by the times in which we live our country has been led step by step to its destruction and extinction by the social vices inherited from the colonial system, and by those produced by twenty-six years of disorder.

The men who have taken roles in the direction of public affairs, lacking both skill and an awareness of the serious obligations placed upon them by the high positions their ambitions have brought them, have been oblivious to the obstacles standing in the way of the welfare and happiness of the nation. This is only natural in a country where men never ascend to power through the will of the people, but always through some type of maneuvering. Sometimes it is accomplished through the intrigues of one party or another, and often by revolutionary action backed by armed force.

The practice of giving government to a people without their consent, which is truly unique for a republic, has meant that the men chosen have never worked in the interests of the people. One reason has been that the parties they represent are concerned only with protecting their own special interests, and have never looked for ability in their candidates, nor the independence that would cause them to think in terms of the national welfare. What they want is men who are firmly tied to their own interests. The men contesting for political power consequently compromise themselves, and are obligated to serve the party that brought them to office.

These are the factors responsible for the fact that some governments give particular protection to the army, others the clergy, others the civil service, and others, finally, all three groups at the same time. But never have we seen a government curb the ambitions of these privileged classes, restrict or eliminate their abuses, nor dedicate themselves to those that are most worthy of the special concern of every worthwhile and patriotic government — the productive classes.[23] For these classes we have had nothing but grandiose promises that have never been fulfilled. Every revolutionist has attempted to discredit the government he wished to overthrow by accusing it of not having protected industry or commerce, and every new government has begun its reign by declaring its first concern to be the promotion of agriculture, commerce, the arts, and so on. These promises, however, have remained in writing only, and have never been implemented. Instead, they have usually been followed by a new set of taxes to satisfy the obligations encountered as a consequence of the new revolution.

It has to be recognized that the workings of this kind of system for a period of twenty-six years have been enough to cause a profound aversion among the laboring classes for their rulers. What bond or sympathy could possibly exist between these people and their government when instead of giving protection it burdens them even more heavily with taxes to satisfy the appetites of the thousands of men from privileged classes who expect to live idly at the expense of the nation? None, of course. Quite the opposite situation exists: troubled and abused classes have with reason come to consider their rulers only as the enemies of their happiness and well being. From unhappy experience, both past and present, they have lost even the remotest hope for the future.

Living in a state of mortal despair that is an inevitable result of their cruel and repeated betrayals, how could these people be expected to sacrifice their few remaining fortunes and their lives for their country? And in defense of what? To ask for such behavior would certainly be to pretend that Mexicans have different emotions than the rest of the world. The times have passed forever in which people will destroy one another at the pleasure of a single man. You can no longer ask any people, let alone those who are fairly knowledgeable, to sacrifice their lives and fortunes in defense of empty phrases. "National honor" is clearly such a vain phrase in a country where the working man is alienated from the rest of society, without the ability to enjoy the fruits of his labor because of the poor administration of justice, where three-fourths or more hope to live from the labor of the rest, where a man cannot travel the highways without a ninety-nine to one chance of being attacked by thieves, where politicians work only to satisfy party ambitions that are always contrary to the interests of the people, where the turmoil caused by the conflicting interests of the privileged classes constantly interfering with the directions of public affairs for their own gain has made a mockery of the more basic principles – or, more accurately, the only ones which can insure the happiness and prosperity of a people, and where for such reasons, finally, the productive classes that have been burdened for a period of twenty-six years with countless hardships, constantly exposed to every kind of frustration, and always mocked by promises that have never been kept, see that their own material interests are in opposition to the rest of society. They have, consequently, no reason to sacrifice themselves in defense of that society.

These powerful considerations are in themselves explanation enough for thoughtful men to understand the apathy with which the majority of the productive class has performed in the present war. It must be added, however, that the Army of the United States has not entered the republic as armies have entered conquered nations before, spreading death and terror in every direction, seizing or destroying the property of its people, violating its women, and victimizing the conquered people. On the contrary, and with the exception of the few individuals that have suffered inevitable hardships when a foreign army crosses into a country in a state of war, the American army, living from its own resources and paying good prices when it has been forced to make requisitions, has respected private property.[24] No peaceful Mexican has been persecuted, everyone has been allowed to continue his business or occupation freely, and instead of the people being burdened with heavy taxes the import duties in occupied ports have been considerably reduced. In the cities and towns of the interior the internal tariff and excise rates have been dropped where they proved injurious to those engaged in the mercantile trade.

In view of all this it is clear that the landowning and laboring classes in Mexico have had no material interests to defend in the present war. To speak frankly, their sympathies have by nature had to be for anything that would end the system of disorder and pillage that has victimized them for so many years. Consequently, to regard the indifference with which they have viewed the present conflict as a special sin of the Mexican race by attributing it to cowardice, weakness, or a complete lack of dignity appears to us to show complete ignorance and lack of perception. There is no doubt that if the laboring classes of any other nation saw themselves oppressed to the extent of ours they would not have been content merely to show indifference, but would have joined the invading army to avenge themselves for their injuries, and to try to improve their own conditions.

There is no need to go to the history of former ages to find support for this argument, for we have seen in our own era that when France wished to eliminate the abuses of the privileged classes thousands of Frenchmen from these classes volunteered to join the ranks of the foreign armies that invaded their country. When Spain was invaded by the armies of Napoleon many eminent Spaniards willingly chose between the cause of civilization and reaction, joined with Joseph Bonaparte, and tried to establish some of the reforms Spanish society needed so badly. Finally, and also in Spain, there was an invasion in 1823 that was welcomed, if not even requested, by all Spaniards of the party of oppression in order to take from the people a constitution whose existence endangered the injustices upon which the privileged classes live.

I have cited these examples only for the purpose of making a brief comparison, and to show that Frenchmen and Spaniards have supported foreign armies invading their own countries with their money and lives. In one instance, near the end of the last century, and in another, in 1823, they sought the protection of foreign bayonets not to free their people from oppression, nor even to improve the condition of a given class, but only to perpetuate the abuses of despotism. Could we then demand of landowning and laboring Mexicans that they invite ruin or death in defense of the very abuses that claim them as victims? In our mind this would be to attempt an absurdity. We are persuaded instead that if industrious Mexicans sacrificed themselves in defense of an order representing nothing but ruin and misery they would richly deserve the ridicule directed against them, for they would have proven that they lacked even the kind of common sense that distinguishes men from brutes.

In spite of these facts the laboring classes of Mexico have given ample proof of their high esteem for the honor and good name of their country. We will not go into the enormous sums they furnished for the Texas war over the space of twelve years, for it is well known that during this period the war gave the government a great excuse to ask for money from everybody without paying it to anybody. It is clear from press reports, however, that during the present year of 1847 alone the government has received millions of pesos in donations, loans, extraordinary contributions, and so on. These sacrifices are even more significant when it is recognized that most of those who made them knew the effort was fruitless, and that there was little hope that their money would go to the cause for which it was given. It was public knowledge, in fact, that while the enemy army advanced unopposed toward the capital some of our generals, colonels, high officials, and other despicable government favorites fought with one another for possession of the little wealth coming into the treasury. Thinking that each peso was perhaps the last the government could collect they rushed to take it with the eagerness of a gang of bandits rushing to steal the watch — or any other item of value — from the body of a dying traveler found lying on the royal highway.

In another situation we have seen the young men of Veracruz join with three or four thousand soldiers, and thinking only of the honor of the land of their birth, defy an army of twelve or fourteen thousand men from within crumbling walls. Bravely and calmly they endured a horrible bombardment that showered the city with more than six thousand projectiles in eighty or ninety hours of fire, causing great destruction and ruin. When they learned that the military chiefs were already engaged in talks with the enemy in order to surrender the city they indignantly threw their now useless arms into the sea rather than surrender them to the conqueror.[25]

There are also many families in Mexico that still weep over the loss of a father, husband, son, or brother in the actions of Churubusco and Molino del Rey; men who paid with their lives for the desire to contribute personally to the defense of Mexico's honor. This is the only motive they could have had, for they had no direct dependence upon the government, nor had they ever received any money in its service. It is true that these examples are not too frequent, but here, as elsewhere, the number of men driven by feelings so noble and generous that they are willing to sacrifice themselves for the honor of others in return for nothing but posthumous fame is necessarily limited.

SECOND PART

With what we have revealed in Part One, we think we have shown clearly that Indians and other groups that comprise the industrious and productive parts of the republic have had no reason to take an interest in the outcome of the war. They have already done much more than could be expected of them, not only in view of the many just grievances they have had against their government, but because the enemy has not directly threatened either their lives or their property.

We must pass now into a consideration of the army, the clergy, and the public employees. Since these three classes actually run the country, and because they are the only ones that have been able to manipulate or benefit from its fortunes, it would follow that in the present struggle they ought to work as for a personal cause, since it is obvious that any new order of enlightenment would undoubtedly bring an end to the abuses from which they have lived. We will nevertheless examine the situation of each of these classes, and we will soon find that if they have been strong enough to prevent the country from changing, and in many ways of contributing to its ruin and destruction, they have not been able to present a united force against the foreign invasion, even though they are convinced that it poses a greater threat to them than to others in our society.

I The Army

We will begin with the army, for this body is undoubtedly the most immediately responsible for our loss of national honor. It has been maintained for defense of this honor during our twenty-six years of independence at a cost to the nation of hundreds of millions of pesos.

We have pointed out in another place that the common soldiers are generally Indians pressed into service by force, and we have also observed that they cannot be expected to have nationalistic feelings, or to take an interest in the preservation of a state of affairs in which they are viewed only as beasts of burden. In respect for the truth, however, we must note that they are very good soldiers, for in addition to a natural bravery they have been hardened by campaign, and we have seen them march hundreds of leagues through bad roads barefooted, poorly clothed and poorly fed, without complaining or committing any significant act of insubordination. It is certain that if these same Indians were led by trained and capable officers they would be as good as soldiers anywhere. The weakness of the Mexican army, therefore, is not in its soldiers, but in its officers who, with few and honorable exceptions, must be the most ignorant and demoralized in the world. It could hardly be otherwise, seeing that military advancement among us has not been a reward for knowledge and recognized valor, but a consequence of gifts and indulgences that mark a most contemptible favoritism.

Immediately upon the consummation of independence the government was besieged by a throng of ignorant and obscure men alleging to have contributed important services and immense sacrifices in the cause of the nation. They asked for high military posts in compensation. Many wanted to be made generals, and only the more modest among them were perhaps satisfied with the rank of colonel. It is true that many of these absurd demands were ignored, but there were many that were honored, and through this procedure men were rapidly brought into the army with no military background; absolutely ignorant of the arts of war, and consequently useless for the career they had chosen to follow. Since that time the abuse in the granting of military titles has been truly scandalous, and it is surprising that some Mexicans are still civilians when so many who have wanted military appointments have obtained them from the government so easily.

Within the past twenty years the favorite occupation of the bulk of the army, except for a few periods, has been to stage revolutions, and disorder in the military has gradually increased. Every new government brought into power by a military revolution, and this includes all of them, has thought that it ought to reward the army faction that elevated it to power, and these rewards have generally consisted of promotions for all generals and officers. The government about to fall, on the other hand, gives promotions to the portion of the army which is faithful to its own cause, and these promotions have always been honored by the new governments so that nobody will be dissatisfied. Because of this every revolution has resulted in a considerable increase in the number of new officers, and an elevation to higher rank for those that already existed. The frequency with which these military farces, called *pronunciamientos,* have been repeated in Mexico should thus not seem strange, because it is obvious that by this route a sub-lieutenant, for instance, who figures in six consecutive revolutions would logically rise to the rank of general.

We can also see by this, which is a point we have noted before, that military rank has not been the reward of intelligence, valor, nor honorable and decent service, but more a matter of compensation for vices expressly condemned in the military code and by all human law. We have, in fact, rewarded with military appointments the base sycophant, the vile denouncer, and many other men for services even more repugnant and contemptible. There have been several instances in which ordinary civilians have been given appointments as colonels in the army. Promotions have been given to the officer who betrayed all his oaths of obedience to the government and deserted his standards in order to join those of the revolution — with the hope, perhaps, of improving his personal finances, and whose crime is not only forgiven, but rewarded upon the success of the revolution. All ideas of morality, subordination, and discipline have consequently disappeared, and without these qualities an army falls into horrible confusion.

In consequence of this disorder, and of the freedom with which appointments and military promotions are awarded, it is not strange that there are in the republic hundreds of generals and thousands of colonels, lieutenant-colonels, and so on, but you can find scarcely a general you would be willing to trust with even a small division. Many of them do not know even the first rudiments of the art of war, and become highly confused if they are put in charge of a company or a patrol. The colonels that could be trusted with a regiment in the field are also limited in number. As far as the junior officers are concerned, very few have any merit, for in addition to their other defects they are generally insubordinate, and this makes them useless for any kind of service.

It must be recognized that it was this kind of army, fighting its first national war against a moderately effective enemy, which cut a figure as ridiculous as that made by the soldiers of the Pope against the hosts of Napoleon. It is, in fact, not difficult to determine the number of defeats suffered by our troops in the present war if one knows first the number of encounters they have had with the enemy, for every battle has by some chance been a defeat – some taking only minutes. But if the military has fared badly in deeds of arms it has not been remiss in giving proclamations, manifestos, and explanations, for in the literary field our army has no equal in the world. It boasts of generals that give impressive speeches to their troops, and to the cities and people they abandon as they march to the rear. Even as they awake in the morning their first action is to issue a proclamation to their valiant fellows in arms. Colonels who have deserted their troops in battle have not lost their positions, for by issuing general manifestos to justify their actions they make everything right. Even junior officers accused by their superiors of deserting their standards in battle have appealed to the public in order to deny the charges against them, or have asked for a suspension of judgment while they gather proof which they will publish in order to keep their honor pure and unblemished. All these suspended judgments, no few in number, have remained embryonic for many years, and will probably remain so until the end of time.

In the midst of the confusion and disorder we have described there are still men in the Mexican army who possess all the knowledge and the honor needed for the noble profession of arms. Some have retired, though, disgusted because of the disorder that exists in the army, or because they are tired of seeing themselves consistently outranked by men whose only advantage is the unmerited favor of the government. Other good men that have remained in the army find greater cause every day to become disgusted with their profession, and have continued in it only because they have no other way to earn a living.

If the matter is considered carefully, there is no encouragement in fact for the intelligent and honorable officer who wishes to fulfill his duty faithfully. In the first place, command of troops is never given to the best and most honored officer, but to the one who best knows how to pander to the government and gain its confidence. The officer that is neither a panderer nor a revolutionary does not succeed in his career, even if he has conducted himself honorably in a hundred battles. The officer that does not pander does not have favor, nor does he have his current pay, and is forced to sell his possessions for a fraction of their value – which is another indictment of the disorder into which government finances have fallen. Then, when it comes to actual fighting, the officer who performed bravely in the face of danger is treated the same as the coward who hid behind the lines, and remained perhaps miles away from the battlefield. This lack of honesty and justice naturally demoralizes every good officer, or perhaps transforms him into a bad one. Hope of reward or fear of punishment, which are the springboards of human action, are simply not recognized in the situation we have described.

In all countries that function normally the officer who dies in battle knows that he leaves his family well provided for under the protection of the government, and if he is incapacitated he can also be certain of a home in which he can spend the rest of his life in comfort and decency. In Mexico this is not so, for although a home for invalids and a pension plan for widows exist in name, a man who is disabled knows that he will die in poverty, spending his final days begging from public charity. If he is killed his family will undoubtedly become destitute – and perhaps fall into consequent prostitution. His corpse, meanwhile, will become food for wolves or vultures, for frequently if not always, nobody bothers to bury those who have fallen on the battlefield.

It is easy to understand how in an army in which the majority of the officers corps is composed of ignorant and corrupt men, and where the honorable and capable officer is discouraged from doing his duty, there is every reason for actions that are ruinous for the country as a whole, but no incentive to defend it from a foreign invasion. We therefore believe that none of the shame which has covered the army in the present struggle can with justice be attributed to special defects of the Mexican race, for it is certain that any army in the world that found itself placed in this kind of disorder and demoralization would, in similar situations, produce the same results. Proof of this fact is found in the pains universally taken to maintain discipline in armies, punishing the slightest infraction with severe penalties, for it is an axiom that "without discipline there is no army."

In the several encounters our troops have had with the invader we have nevertheless come to identify the few good generals and officers we had in the army. Some have been left dead on the field of battle, others have been wounded, and others have been made prisoner because they have remained in positions their duty demanded. Even from the enemy they have received all the considerations due a brave and honored officer who succumbs after having loyally lived up to all his obligations to the country.

II The Clergy

We pass now to an examination of the clergy. It owns the majority of the real property across the republic, and from this has come the great and tragic influence it has had upon society. It seemed natural that its members would rally strongly in defense of the nation — or, more accurately, in defense of their own property — convinced that any new and even halfway intelligent government would deprive them of their immense wealth, and restrict them to the simple exercise of the purely spiritual mission on earth. An even greater reason for resisting the advance of the enemy army is in the fact that it represents a country in which an absolute toleration of religions is one of the fundamental bases of the social system. It was evident that if Mexico succumbed in the struggle the clergy here would not only face the loss of its property, but also of the unique and absolute power it exercises in a country such as this, where other religions are not tolerated.

Given these reasons, the selfishness of the clergy relative to a cause it should view as its own can come only from two factors. The first is the ignorance of its members, who are certainly not equal to the difficult age in which they live, and whose ignorance prevents them from foreseeing the future consequences of their stupid and selfish conduct. Second, and even more important, is the inequality of wealth among the various members of this privileged class. While a small number of them live in the midst of greatest abundance the rest have hardly enough for a decent subsistence. We shall examine the inequality that exists among the different classes that make up the clergy, and the accuracy of this observation will quickly become apparent.

The Mexican clergy is composed of bishops and capitulars, priests and vicars, private priests, or chaplains, and monastics of both sexes. The bishops and capitulars, who form what is known as the high clergy, are supported by tithes. Their income has been much reduced now that the working class is no longer forced to tithe by law, but the amount still paid is considerable. It is calculated by knowledgeable persons that the income of the Archbishop of Mexico today approaches some hundred thousand pesos a year, and that of the poorest bishop in the republic is not less than ten thousand. Inasmuch as the portion of the tithes allocated to the Archbishop and bishops is less than half the total sum, it can be easily calculated that the remainder gives the canons and capitulars an income that is not to be despised.

While in the large cities, such as Mexico, Puebla, Guadalajara, Querétaro, Orizaba, and others, there are hosts of clerics that serve nobody, and while bishops and canons spend their comfortable and ordered lives free from problems amid all the pleasures a good life can give, the priests and vicars, who actually do more for the real cause of religion, generally find their lives to be filled with labor, and even misery. We will quote what Dr. Mora says about village priests in his work *Mexico and Its Revolutions,* for nothing we could say would more clearly reveal the situation of this important segment of the clergy:

> The curates of Mexico administer over the sacraments and parochial functions, [he says], and even the best situated are always considerably overworked. A parish priest never has an hour to himself, nor a minute

of rest. He is subject to call in order to comfort the ill at a moment's notice, often traveling a considerable distance through the heaviest rains, the worst heat of the torrid zone, or the rigors of the cold. He must conduct funerals, baptisms, and weddings, and keep records of them all. Unlike everyone else, he is unable to rest even on holidays because of the heavy burden of duties that force him into many painful miles of travel in order to say mass at points separated great distances from one another. His interests, and even his health, are in conflict with his duty, for upon him exclusively falls the entire weight of the burden of the holy ministry. And what is the reward for such hardships — and for the endless and useful labors? Contributions that are insignificant in amount and humiliating to try to collect, for to speak of parish dues is to speak of everything that is futile in the way of a contribution. The parish priest has no other income than the donations he receives from funerals, baptisms, and weddings. Any others, as from feast days, meetings, masses, etc., are haphazard and dependent upon the violition of the faithful, which cannot be counted on — particularly in these days — for attachment to these practices has diminished noticeably.

Private clerics are those who are not tied to any special ecclesiastical service. They are known as chaplains because they subsist, or are supposed to subsist, from special funds established through private donations for this purpose, called chaplaincies. The total value of these funds throughout the republic is considerable, since it is the principal source of pious works which, according to lowest estimates, approached a value of eighty million pesos in the year 1804. The way these funds are dispensed, however, is another matter. Each chaplaincy contains three thousand pesos, which produces an interest of one hundred and fifty pesos a year. This is not enough to sustain a cleric with any decency in Mexico, for such a small sum will not even pay for his food. The granting of these chaplaincies is a function of the Archbishop or the bishops in their respective dioceses, and the function is abused because each rewards his favorites. There are some clerics — and even those who are not clerics — who enjoy the income from four, six, or more chaplaincies, while others have but one.[26] The latter, who are in the majority, spend their lives in great privation, and are only able to get what else they need for their subsistence from whatever alms they receive from various individuals in the performance of a certain number of masses or for some other religious services. These alms grow more scarce each day because of the general poverty, and for other reasons which cannot be explained here.

As far as the religious corporations of both sexes are concerned, it is true that there are some that are genuinely poor and live from public charity, but the majority are very wealthy. Their immense holdings form a principal part of the wealth of the clergy in the republic. The fate of the individual, however, is no happier in the rich convents than in the poor, since in all of them it is the few that enjoy the wealth simply because they control it, and the rest get only what is necessary to live in some degree of poverty.

In convents for friars, for instance, the men that prosper are the provincial, the prior, and those who have charge of the administration of the convent properties, but the others in the community have no more than their cells, their meals in the refectory, and whatever alms they receive for saying special masses. In the case of the nuns, and no matter how wealthy the convent, no more than four or five pesos a week are given to each nun for her expenses. This small stipend provides assurance that the wealth of the convents will never diminish, since it is no more than a small interest on the capital each of them paid when they entered the congregation. The nuns that actually benefit from the wealth of the convents are the Mother Superiors. They are first given a comfortable house by the convent itself, which they inhabit free. They also get a substantial commission on rental incomes, and, most importantly, they have the perquisites that the administration of such extensive interests necessarily produces. The chaplain and sexton in each convent also prosper, for they have very good salaries, and are also continually being given gifts of all sorts by the nuns.

It can be seen by this account that although more than half of the real property in the republic belongs to the clergy the benefits from this wealth — and of its related abuses — are enjoyed by only a fraction of this privileged class, while the majority of its members have scarcely enough to live. At the same time, while one part carries the entire burden of the priestly function the other lives in idleness, enjoying the good life. This inequality, which originates in the institution itself, is sustained and intensified by the favoritism that exists within the ecclesiastical governments in the various dioceses. It naturally engenders disgust and even hatred among people within the organization, which destroys all sense of union and espirit de corps, and these are what give real force and power to every society or corporation. Unity and espirit de corps can exist only in a community in which all benefit from its advantage with some degree of equality. But what interest in the preservation of its abuses, and of the great wealth amassed to benefit only some individuals among its clergy, can those have who participate in neither of them? What direct interest can a village priest have, for instance, in the continued collection of tithes, or in the conservation of the extensive wealth of convents for monks and nuns? None, certainly, for they have nothing to do with these things, nor do the private clergy.

It should not be thought that we intend in any way to defend the clergy for the cold selfishness they have shown in the present national struggle. We have made these observations only to demonstrate that there is no unity among the clergy in the republic, nor, given the inequality that exists in the fortunes of its members, could there be. Neither have they been able to motivate themselves to work together in defense of the same cause.

It has also been our object to demonstrate that not all of the members of the clergy, but only the smallest part of them, can with justice be called criminal for their indifference in the present contest. As we see it, crime exists principally among the so-called high clergy, and among all the others that trade and prosper with the management of the immense wealth that is so improperly controlled by the Church. These men are criminals; not only for their selfishness in the present circumstances, but because they are so much the source of all the misfortunes of the nation. They have controlled the personnel of every government we have had since independence in order to block any reform that might put their absurd power in danger. They have exercised their perverse influence on society to keep it static, ignorant, and embrutalized, because this is the only way they continue to enjoy all their malpractices and privileges without opposition. They have employed a part of the wealth that they claim to be for God and for the worship of God in fomenting immorality throughout the nation, provoking several revolutions in order to overthrow each government that is not in agreement with their always self-interested views. Last year they made every effort, in conjunction with General Paredes, to plant a monarchy here with a European prince, and they hoped to see their Christian tribunal of the Inquisition re-established in order to put every Mexican who would not meekly submit to their power under penalty.[27] Finally, while the houses and temples of Veracruz were being flattened by the guns of the invading army last March, and while hundreds of Mexicans died on the battlefield defending our national honor, they created a scandalous spectacle in the capital of the republic, which was provoked and sustained with the Church's money. Mexicans killed one another, not because of a religion they did not profess, and which no one attacked, but in defense of the money requested from the clergy by the government to fight the war, and which it did not wish to give – for money is the great object of its worship and adoration.[28]

Because of these factors we have not the slightest intentions of exonerating the group that makes up the clerical aristocracy. We detest their mundane views, their sordid avarice, and their malevolent influence upon our society. We can only compare the contempt we have for them with the respect and veneration inspired by the modest, virtuous and sagacious priest who professes without hypocrisy or ostentation the true religion of Jesus Christ. Pursuing the purpose we laid out for this study, we will limit ourselves simply to a rejection of the opinion that the conduct of this segment of the clergy is a defect peculiar to Mexicans. Every person that is not completely ignorant well knows that the general history of the clergy from the time it dropped its purely religious character and converted itself into a body politic is a history of selfishness and criminal actions committed in the sacred name of religion; and that if it has always tried to extort as many advantages as it could from a society it has never consented to respond with a sacrifice of the wealth it has acquired.

III Government Officials

The history of our civil service is quite similar to that of the military. In the perpetual disorder and mishandling of our government, appointments have been given out in great profusion in response to the recommendation of one important person or another, or to reward the most contemptible service lent to some individual within the government. Only rarely has the integrity or the ability of an appointee been considered when an appointment is made. The only factor usually considered is whether the person who recommends him has any influence, in which case the appointment is made promptly, and without further investigation. There have also been instances in which officials already of some importance promoted their careers by continuing to pay money to someone located near the center of government, thus receiving their favor.

One result of the laxity in granting appointments is that there are many officials in public tax offices that are not only ignorant of the grammar of their own idiom, and even arithmetic, but that do not know how to write their own language. Morality is another issue, and the cases of officials that have made immense fortunes through illegal abuses of the trust placed in them by the government are as numerous as they are scandalous. The corruption among this class is so well organized and commonly accepted by society that no one is shocked to observe an official that makes a salary of only two or three thousand pesos a year buy a hacienda, fill his house with the most exquisite and costly furniture, and maintain his family in extraordinary luxury. None of this attracts attention because such cases are so numerous, and the public is used to seeing all officials that have anything to do with the handling of public revenues — with a few notable exceptions — spend three or four times their salary.

In spite of the scandalous corruption and ineptitude of the majority of the officials the government, even when willing, is helpless to apply a remedy. According to the laws of the republic the official who has received a government appointment acquires what is defined as tenure in his employment, and nobody, not even the government itself, can discharge him without previous formation of cause. Given the state of the administration of justice in our country, this condition is equivalent to agreeing that officials can do as they please without fear of losing their positions.

It is true that there have been some instances in which officials have been suddenly removed by the government, but these removals have invariably been temporary, with the appointments being renewed shortly afterward through a weakness that characterizes all of our governments. In other instances, when the government's reasons for the discharge are more serious, the discharged official is always welcomed by the opposition party, and its periodicals immediately begin a clamor about the horrible offense committed by the government in attacking the tenure of an official without respect to the formulas established by law. The government responsible for the action is called arbitrary, despotic, and tyrannical. The grossest epithets and lies are employed to bring it into disrepute, and to make it appear criminal for an act that was perhaps one of the purest justice. Because the government always represents the weakest part of society, and because the men who run it live in fear of attacks from the press, the only way to silence this intolerable outcry is to reappoint the aggrieved official to his post and to forget about discharging him even if someone again finds the same or worse reasons for doing so.

From what has been said it will become apparent that the best thing a person can aspire toward in Mexico is to be a government official, and the offices would be true sinecures if it were not that the excessive number of officials has prejudiced the class in general. In every orderly country offices are created only to the extent that they can be supported by revenue. In Mexico, however, where everything is done in reverse, they create public revenue for the officials. The abuse of creating offices has been such that in addition to the growing number needed for every department because of a complicated system of bookkeeping, there are many positions that cost the treasury four or five salaries. Although only one individual actually fills the position another three or four are declared to be pensioners or supernumeraries, with full pay, in order to place some favorite of the government on the payroll. This has necessarily resulted in having more officials than can be sustained, and only those that have special influence are appointed or made supernumeraries to certain offices in which they punctually receive their salary or more. All the rest receive only enough to live on miserably, or perhaps even nothing. This inequality would be unjust and detestable even if it were committed among people of equal worth. It is even more hateful when, as often happens, the favored officials given such preference are not men of the greatest honor, service, or ability.

For all these reasons it can be seen that among government officials, as among the military and the clergy, espirit de corps neither does nor could exist. Although they are strong enough to cause injuries of great consequence throughout society there is not the stimulus of personal interest among them that would enable them all to work together, not even in defense of the abuses from which they live.

IV Conclusion

We have concluded the melancholy description of the state in which all classes of society throughout the republic are found, and it is certainly an unhappy task, particularly for a Mexican, to paint a picture of his country without being able to present anything favorable. We are writing in Mexico, however, where we have thousands of witnesses, and instead of being contradicted we believe we have omitted many ingredients that would have made the picture of our unhappy situation even blacker and more dreadful. We would be happy to be proven wrong, for we are Mexicans, and there is nothing we want more than to see our nation happy and respected the world over. But this does not give us illusions, and in the picture we have drawn of our society we do not believe we have used anything but undeniable facts, for they are visible to anyone willing to see the reality of things without passion or self-deception.

It appears futile for foreign writers to wear themselves out searching for an effeminacy or degradation in the Mexican race for the indifference it has shown in the present war, just as it is ridiculous for Mexicans to try to blame one another now for what has happened. As far as we are concerned it can all be explained in these few short words: *In Mexico there has not been, nor could there have been, a national spirit, for there is no nation.* If a nation cannot call itself such unless it has all the elements to bring happiness and well being internally and respect from abroad, Mexico cannot call itself a nation.

It would be useless to assert that Mexico has an immense territory of more than one hundred and twenty thousand square leagues, bordered by great seas, with a multitude of navigable rivers, with the most varied climates that permit the production of any crop in the world, whose astonishing fertility gives the farmer back a hundred times the seed he plants, and where, to crown the wealth that has blessed this soil, there are great hills and mountains filled with precious metals. All this only proves that this country has all the natural elements needed to produce a great and prosperous nation, and that with the passage of time a people will inhabit this land that will undoubtedly occupy one of the first places among the richest and most powerful nations on the earth. But while fanatacism, ignorance, and indolence continue as the basis of our education, and while we do not have a truly honest and active government to accomplish all the reforms this society needs to begin moving, the Mexican people, even though surrounded by gold and silver, will be a weak and unfortunate people. They will continue to present the same unhappy spectacle as that of a beggar plagued by misery and hunger and covered with rags living in a beautiful palace filled with gold and every type of wealth, none of which he knows how to make use of for his own happiness and well being.

A nation is nothing more than a great family, and in order for it to be stable and strong it means that all its members must be closely united with ties of interest and affections of the heart. In Mexico this union is not possible, and all it takes to convince a person of this is to take a quick look at the different classes that make up our hapless society. In addition, a civil war that has been with us constantly for a period of thirty-six years has demoralized every class of society. It has also destroyed the only principle of order this country had at the time of its independence, which was the respect and blind obedience to authority that furnished the basis of the colonial system. This respect and obedience have been replaced by license and the most scandalous irresponsibility. Freedom of the press, which is rightfully utilized elsewhere to enlighten the people, is used here to demoralize and brutalize them more every day. Instead of attacking various abuses and prejudices, instead of giving news on matters vital to society and advocating reforms needed for the prosperity and happiness of the country frankly, firmly, and with good faith, the periodicals, with few exceptions, have constantly trafficked in the basest and most destructive passions. They stir up hatreds, mislead public opinion, and play alternately with the interests of the classes that live from public abuses and the ignorance of the general public.

Moving to another problem, we find that in the endless succession of governments over the past twenty-six years the leaders of all parties have established reputations for inefficiency or corruption. People have become accustomed to holding disrespect for their authorities, and instead of identifying them with wisdom and virtue they see only weakness and vice. Everyone consequently hates and despises them, and none inspire general confidence. In our endless domestic problems they have all more or less tarnished themselves, and have lost the little prestige they had. Some have done it through their dishonesty, and others by demonstrating a complete inability to direct public affairs effectively or to get to the heart of the problems that plague the republic. As is natural, the general and permanent suffering of society has brought these men the hatred of its members.

Different groups within our society are divided into factional organizations with one kind of political princples or another, and every one of these parties believes or pretends that its opponents are the only cause of the country's misfortunes.[29] They all sustain their own opinions with such emotionalism that they would seemingly view the total loss of the country with less feeling than the triumph of a party other than their own. In the whirlwind of passions and verbal confusion emanating from the parties themselves all truth has disappeared, leaving in its place the most contemptible charlatanism. Every man has his plan for everyone else, and proposes to make the country happy through his own ideas. In the midst of the resulting babble the Mexican republic presents a strange spectacle in which all men speak the same language, but nobody understands anybody. The only men capable of taking advantage of this situation are those that have no political convictions, and they gain their livelihood by playing upon the general disorder itself.

For all these reasons Mexicans are badly divided, and they are less capable of understanding each other than the inhabitants of Saint Petersberg and Cape Horn. There are almost no two men who are in accord in their political opinions, for even those who agree on the questions of ends disagree about the means of obtaining them. What kind of resistance could a people offer in this state of dissolution? None, certainly, and we again say that it is vain to look for the cause of the misfortunes of the republic in special defects of its race, for the cause stems from nothing but vicious education and poor organization. Mexico has succumbed in the same way it has succumbed before, and the way people will always succumb when they are poorly educated and governed. There are many examples of this throughout the history of the world, and the misfortune the Mexican republic now suffers is a new and severe lesson for all nations. We hope particularly that it will not be lost upon other South American republics, for they are similar to us in respect to origin, education, and even social problems.

A person might conclude that there is something shameful in the fact that even though Mexicans consummated their independence twenty-six years ago they still have not been able to organize themselves in a stable and productive manner, and that instead of prospering under self-government they are today more impoverished, more divided, and consequently weaker than on the day they threw off the colonial yoke. There is some apparent validity in this charge, and it is for this reason that we hear it rather generally repeated that Mexicans do not have the capacity to govern themselves. Many also assert that there is no cure for this incapacity. According to some it is a result of the climate, while others attribute it to defects in our physical makeup. We reject such absurd contentions with the contempt they deserve, and we do not hesitate to identify them for what they are. We are firmly convinced that everything that has happened in Mexico from the time of its independence until today is precisely what would have had to happen without any of the defects attributed to the Mexican race. If one cares to examine the social problems with which Mexico began its career as an independent nation impartially he will instead have to agree that any other people with the same problems would by now have shocked the world with even bloodier and more horrible scenes.

The remark of the magistrate Bataller[30] at the time independence was achieved is still often quoted in Mexico as a prophetic statement: "You could not give the Mexicans a greater punishment," he said, "than that of self-government." The good judge certainly did not have to wrack his brains long in order to deliver this terrible sentence, for only a slight knowledge of the society of New Spain was enough for one to be able to predict that self-government would necessarily be painful for whatever time was necessary for all the vices and prejudices that had become so strongly rooted in their education and their customs to disappear.

What, in fact, was the society of Mexico at the time of independence? We must first exclude from consideration the four million or more Indians, for in their semi-savage state they could scarcely be considered as part of society. What of the education and customs of the other part, which was considered to be advanced? Of the three million or so people in Mexico of European or mixed race eighteen-twentieths could not read nor write, and this alone conveys the impression that the nation and its people did not belong to the civilized world. Society was dominated by a clergy that generally lacked education and virtue, but that was sufficiently astute and avaricious so that in three hundred years of fanaticism it had made itself master of the greater part of the real property in the nation. In addition to the influence it enjoyed through the possession of its immense wealth it had a monopoly over the education of youth in its schools, pulpits, and confessionaries, where it disseminated ideas meant to cement its power more strongly each day. Not content with this, it burrowed into the bosom of families in order to watch and control even the most secret actions of private life. It thus converted itself into a censor of all their activities, not infrequently abusing the confidence accorded to it because of its role, to commit acts condemned by both morals and religion. It was a clergy, finally, that believed in the right to influence and even direct public affairs, and then claimed that it was dependent upon neither the government nor the nation itself, for under the pretense of its divine mission on earth it declared itself independent of all human authority. It was easy to foresee that a country left with the inheritance of such a monstrous institution had a problem that would keep it in a state of misery for a long time. The power of this privileged group, which is founded upon the ignorance and prejudice of the people in general, is a tremendous power than can be diminished only through knowledge. But to educate a people anew and to make it change its customs is not an effort of a few years, particularly when the clergy itself works to impede this.

Under the influence of the clergy Mexicans learned to believe that religion did not consist in the modest practice of virtue, but in meaningless externals. They were taught that one cannot be a good man nor a respectable woman unless they contributed frequently to the Church — even if this meant neglecting their homes and families. The man that filled his house with images of saints and that attended mass daily and went to confession and communion monthly was taken to be an exemplary man, even if he practiced the most shameful vices in his private life. Hypocrisy was thus canonized in Mexico as the finest of virtues, and sincerity was treated as a vice. The clergy was convinced that along with civilization would come the end of the abuses upon which it based its power, so it infused among the people a profound hatred of foreigners, inducing the masses to believe that all outsiders were heretics.

The people under the principal care of the republic were submerged in hopeless misery, which resulted in an abject and brutish condition that was then perpetuated. Accustomed to an idle and slothful life, their favorite diversions were bullfights, the almost daily religious processions, pilgrimages, novenas, and, finally, the gambling houses and taverns where they passed the time in gambling and drunkeness. It is clear that a people dedicated to such pastimes must be a degraded people, constantly lacking the means not only to feed themselves, but even to cover their nudity. This type of people nevertheless formed three-fourths of the total population of New Spain at the time of independence. The wealthy classes in the country, which consisted of some counts, marquises, and other titled nobles, landowners, ranchers, and merchants, had educations that were no more impressive, and it was generally true that they could be distinguished from the vulgar only by their dress and because they could read, write and count with some facility. Other than that it is likely that the only books to pass through their hands were those of their respective business affairs, the almanac, the catechism of Father Ripalda,[31] the *Lives of the Saints,* and one devotionary or another. What was referred to as the Mexican nobility surpassed even the general public with its own particular brand of ignorance, so much so that the titles of count, marquis, esquire, etc., were synonymous here with "stupid" and "ignorant."

It should not seem strange that there would be such ignorance among these classes, for knowledge was useless in the uneventful and monotonous life of those that lived in the colony. This was particularly true for the Mexicans, as the entire direction of public affairs, and all the offices of any importance in society, were always discharged by Spaniards. The only things Mexicans therefore had to learn were to obey and be silent. They were never to discuss politics, let alone religious matters. These were very dangerous subjects, for it was known that where the king and the Inquisition were involved you had to be careful. For such a purely vegetable life learning and knowledge were useless, and all that was needed was enough money to furnish the greatest possible enjoyment through material things.

In general the Spaniards who came to live in the colony were honest and industrious, but they were also fanatical and ignorant, and they were consequently unable to pass on to their children ideas that they had not held themselves. This still would have been acceptable if they had taught them their own good habits and their love of work, but instead almost all of them had the foolish desire to train their sons as gentlemen. They made them go to college, bought them some captaincy in the army, or placed them in some government office, because it was a matter of pride that their sons should not have to work as they had. From these mistaken ideas, which became part of their education, came the contempt that the majority of Mexicans in the so-called decent class had for commerce, agriculture, and the useful arts. From such ideas also came the search for appointments and rage for public office that caused and continue to cause so much harm to this society.

The most knowledgeable class Mexico had was among the men who had some learned profession, such as lawyers, doctors, etc., but even they were far from really being able to consider themselves knowledgeable.

In the colleges, [says Zavala],[32] they taught Medieval Latin, the canons, and they taught scholastic theology and polemics, so that young people filled their heads with eternal and unintelligible arguments over grace, middle knowledge,[33] the processions of the Trinity, and bodily ascension. These were all as useless as they were effective in making young people vain, prideful, and disputatious about matters they did not understand. What passed for philosophy was a tissue of nonsense about primary matter, syllogistic forms, and the other abstractions taken from Aristolelian philosophy poorly interpreted by the Arabs. The theory of heavenly bodies was wrongly depicted in order to discredit the true system of Copernicus, against which the Inquisition and the Vatican launched their attacks. No useful truth, no principle, no idea capable of inspiring noble or generous feelings was heard in those Jesuit schools.[34] They ignored the names of the masters of the philosophy of truth, and Saint Thomas, Scotus, Belarmino, Mother Agreda, and other writers as freakish as these were put in the hands of the youth, who knew absolutely nothing of Bacon, Berulamio, Newton, Galileo, Locke, and Condillac. They did not know that there was such a science as political economics, while Voltaire, Volney, Rousseau, D'Alembert, etc. were declared by the teachers to be monsters sent to their just rewards by Divine

Providence. The works of these and other philosophers never penetrate Latin American shores.

The zeal of the Inquisitors was superior to the cupidity of the merchants of New Spain, and as the latter were all fanatic and ignorant Spaniards who also had other means of income they never attempted to introduce foreign products that might arouse the jealousy of the clergy or the censure of the authorities. The principal interest of these groups coincided with those of the court: to maintain a state of abjectness and stupification among the inhabitants of the New World in order to profit from its immense wealth, and to govern without opposition.

We have already commented on the lack of education in Mexican society at the time of independence, and we ought to add that the examples the Spanish government had given to the Mexicans at the time of independence in respect to the science of good government and the handling of public affairs were equally harmful. Mexicans were quite familiar with the scandals that took place in the court of Madrid, where one could obtain any kind of appointment or favor by using gold or personal influence. This was particularly noticeable when people came to fill various important posts for which they were obviously not qualified. But even when the inhabitants of New Spain might have ignored this they had additional examples before them of the profit made from the Viceregal power in the times of Branciforte, Iturrigaray, and others.[35] There are still some men walking the streets of Mexico, now grey headed, that can cite from whom, to whom, in what way, and for how much money public offices were sold in those days. Many more witnesses are still around that were present at certain banquets where groups of people employed in the public tax offices gathered together and secretly lost hundreds or thousands of ounces of gold in games of chance. With few exceptions almost all the viceroys, *audiencia* judges, and other officials of any rank returned to Spain after a few years in the colony with their fortunes already made, the size depending upon what luck they had enjoyed. It is common knowledge that Viceroy Branciforte alone, whom we mentioned before, made his return to the Peninsula with more than two million pesos. Everyone knew that the administration of justice was easily inclined to one side or another, not by the weight of reason, but by that of gold or other considerations. It was also public knowledge that for the man who wanted to obtain something from the court in Madrid it was as if he were in Rome: he accomplished nothing, no matter how deserving his request, if he was not supported by money and favorable endorsement by influential people. The completion of a dismal social education came through the tumultuous expulsion of the Viceroys Iturrigaray and Apodoca, which instilled within Mexicans the unfortunate lesson that governments could be overthrown through uprisings by the armed forces.[36]

It was easy to foresee that a country such as this, where indolence, vice, fanaticism, prejudice, and ignorance formed the basis of public knowledge, would have many years of suffering before it could get on its feet. What made this even more certain was the large number of problems that lay rooted in the very ignorance of the people. It was obvious that they were having a difficult struggle just in keeping themselves alive, and that for a long time their plight would constitute an insuperable obstacle to the establishment of any more balanced and intelligent new order of things. Can Mexicans thus be legitimately blamed for the way things are today?

The work of independence — that is, the destruction of the Viceregal government by force — was the easiest part of a daring enterprise, for it was a simple deed of arms that required nothing more than audacity and valor enough to fight. Once that deed was accomplished the most difficult part of the task remained, which was the political regeneration of society. This could happen only through the creation of a government that was genuinely dedicated to the future happiness and prosperity of the nation. It had to be willing to take every necessary action to educate and inspire the people, correct or destroy all the abuses and privileges that remained from the colonial system, remove the shackles from agriculture and commerce (which are the only sources of wealth, power, and knowledge among nations), and, finally, to open a friendly door to worthy men everywhere who wanted to settle among us, recognizing that the greatest need of this underpopulated country was to build a sizeable population of active and industrious people. Through their actions and industry these people would fructify all the many and rich gifts placed in their hands by the God of nature. If this had happened the fortunes of the republic would undoubtedly be different today. But in order to undertake these reforms we needed men of great wisdom; men that stood above prejudice, and who possessed the determination and courage of conviction to dedicate themselves to the happiness and aggrandizement of their own country. Men such as this could have obtained these goals without succumbing to the selfish interests of individuals or corporations, but this type of man neither did nor could exist in colonial society. There have been some since that have attempted several important reforms at different times, but none have succeeded. They have been blocked by a combination of the selfishness of the privileged classes on one side, and the passions of a general public steeped in ignorance on the other. The country has consequently gone further every day toward its ruin and total extinction.

It should not be concluded from our description of the education and customs of the inhabitants of New Spain that it is our purpose to offend the Spaniards or their government, for we have no such intention. Our only object in giving an accurate picture of what Mexico was at the time of independence, and what it has been since, is to reveal the actual reasons for this country's inability to govern itself effectively, or to defend itself in the present war with the United States. We are confident that with all we have shown in this study we have accomplished our purpose, even though this type of publication demands brevity and conciseness. When the main causes of its misfortunes are viewed impartially Mexico merits anything but the contempt and scorn of other nations. It deserves instead the understanding due an unfortunate people whose misfortunes are falsely ascribed by some to racial defects, but who actually suffer from a combination of tragic circumstances which have reduced society to the sorry state in which ours is found today.

On another subject, we have no desire to raise the slightest animosity toward the Spaniards, and we view the repeated insults that

Mexicans and Spaniards have traded for the past twenty-six years as a matter of ridiculous folly. In our belief the Spanish have no reason to wish ill to Mexicans for making themselves independent from the mother country, for the desire for independence is a natural feeling among all men, and to follow this impulse cannot be viewed as a crime. Neither do Mexicans have any reason to hate the Spanish for the bad education and customs they left here, for it is a universally recognized principle of justice that you cannot demand more of someone than they can give, and the Spaniards could not carry other ideas or customs than those which they had themselves and which, to the misfortune of the Peninsula, had dominated there since the reign of Phillip II. But we have seen with positive contempt the reports in some Madrid newspapers this year telling of the triumphs obtained by the North American army in Mexico against little or no resistance from this country, and informing their readers that they are ashamed to have anything in common with Mexicans. It would be much more legitimate for all of us who form part of the Spanish family to take shame at the sight of the backwardness and misery found wherever the beautiful Spanish idiom is spoken, in the Old World as well as the New. Instead of trading mutual insults which no one can prove and which help no one, we ought to work in good faith in each of our respective countries to eliminate the ignorance, fanaticism, and other barbarities found there today.

As far as Mexico is concerned, however, the main problem is the tragic situation which it finds itself in at the present moment. Exhausted and without the means to fight, with an invading army that has already seized its ports, its principal sources of income, and even the capital itself, and with a refugee government that lacks resources, prestige, and is unable to take measures necessary to uphold the rights and honor of the nation, it is easy to predict that the final act of this tragic drama will be a treaty of peace.[37] It is also easy to predict that this treaty will be highly damaging and shameful for Mexico, and that we will lose a large part of our territory to indemnify the victorious enemy for the war he has had the grace to bring us. Once that treaty has been concluded it can also be predicted that national independence will not be an empty phrase for us from that time on, but a mockery; an ironic joke. It is certain that after the specacle we have produced from our weakness – or, more accurately, from our impotence – our political life as a nation will become more unstable and precarious every day.

With this tragic conviction, our only wish at this point is that all the abuse and damage we have suffered in this war will produce a salutory awakening among all Mexicans. Most importantly, the men who have some influence in society and in the direction of public affairs need to become convinced that we must change paths, for the one we have followed until now has obviously led us to the edge of an abyss. If this happens, the war, although a tragedy right now, will undoubtedly be a blessing in the future, and society will be widely compensated later for the injuries it has just received. We can at least entertain the hope that even though our country will be much diminished in territory it will govern itself under a well reasoned system of liberty and knowledge, and will soon have the self-esteem that exists in other civilized nations. Instead of walking in foreign countries with heads inclined as Mexicans do today, denying their origin or blushing when they do reveal it, perhaps in the future we or our children will be able to give the name of the country without shame.

But if, as we fear, we have learned nothing from the hard lesson we have received; if we continue to do everything as we have done it before; if the ruinous interests of individuals or corporations continue to dominate the true interests of the country; if the army and government officials continue to act as tyrants and sadists instead of as servants of society; if the clergy continues to interfere in national politics in order to maintain the status quo; if the government continues to think only of today, and never considers tomorrow; if the administration of justice goes on as it has until now, and criminals continue to pass triumphantly through society; if industry and commerce, instead of being protected, continue to be penalized through heavy and unjust taxes in order to support a multitude of idlers who wish to live without working; if the public debt continues in its present chaos in order to satisfy the greed of wretched and avaricious speculators instead of getting an arrangement that would transform it into an element that would be conducive to order and prosperity; if the same hostile ideas that we have had in respect to foreigners continue to reign, which prohibit them from ever settling freely among us or of taking any interest in the progress or improvement of the country; and if we continue with our usual *pronunciamientos,* destroying and erecting a government every three months in order to satisfy the malcontents who propose to live from disorder, and whose number has grown prodigiously because of the impunity those who disturb the public peace enjoy here; then it will be absolutely necessary for all Mexicans who are sensible and who have something to lose to accept one truth, no matter how hard it may be. That truth will be that we can no longer go alone as a nation, and that we will need, at least for a period of some years, the aid or armed intervention of some foreign nation. Once persuaded of this fact, the only question remaining is whether it would be better if that aid comes from the United States, with its democratic principles, or from some of the European monarchies. Would to God that after all the calamities we have already suffered we will have the good judgment needed so that we never reach the point at which we have to take that humiliating extreme as the only means of our salvation!

Mexico, December 1847. *Several Mexicans*

REFERENCES

1 José Fernando Ramírez, *Mexico During the War with the United States,* Walter V. Scholes, ed., Elliott P. Scherr, trans., *University of Missouri Studies,* XXIII. No. 1 (Columbia, 1950), 103.

2 See Charles Hale, *Mexican Liberalism in the Age of Mora,* 1821-1853 (New Haven, 1968), 13-14, 33, 207, 283; and Jesús Reyes Heroles, *El liberalismo mexicano,* Tomo II, *La sociedad fluctuante* (Mexico, 1958), 370-88.

3 The liberal movement had divided into two wings, and though they differed little in terms of basic ideology each had its own attitude toward the question of reform. The group called *exaltados,* or *puros,* was the most radical in approach, demanding immediate implementation of the liberal reform program, including confiscation of Church properties and secularization of the educational system. The *moderados* or moderates, had a more gradualist approach, were perhaps more concerned about property rights, and less democratically oriented. They tended to regard the *puros* as irresponsible and demogogic, while the *puros* often questioned the sincerity of *moderado* commitment to reform.

4 Jesús Reyes Heroles, for instance, who has edited a collection of Otero's writing, was certain enough of its authorship to include this essay among the selections. He admits that the pamphlet may have been the work of more than one man. Even so, he adds, "it can be asserted with confidence . . . that Mariano Otero was among them, and that he played a decisive part in its writing." See Mariano Otero, *Obras,* Recopilación selección, comentarios y estudio preliminar de Jesús Reyes Heroles, Tomo I (Mexico, 1967), 96. The pamphlet appears on pp. 97-137 of the same volume.

5 See Antonio de la Peña y Reyes, ed., *Algunos documentos sobre el Tratado de Guadalupe y la situación de México durante la invasión americana* (Mexico, 1930), 69-92.

6 Francisco Suarez Iriarte, *Defensa Pronunciada ante el gran jurado el* 21 *de marzo de* 1850, *por Francisco Suarez Iriarte* (Mexico, 1850), 24.

7 For an account of this episode see Dennis E. Berge, "A Mexican Dilemma: The Mexico City Ayuntamiento and the Question of Loyalty, 1846-1848," *Hispanic American Historical Review,* L (May, 1970), 229-56.

8 A personalized biographical sketch of Otero, as well as an account of his death, can be found in Guillermo Prieto, *Memorias de mis tiempos* (Mexico, 1958), 497-99.

9 In addition to *El siglo diez y nueve,* Morales wrote for *El Hombre Libre, La Gaceta, El aguila mexicano, El Monitor, El Democratico, El Republicano,* and *Los Debates,* which he also edited; see Marcos Arróniz, *Manual de biografía mejicana, ó galería de hombres célebre de méjico* (Paris, 1857), 236-40.

10 Jesús Rodriguez Frausto, *Juan Bautista Morales* (Guanajuato 1956), n.p.

11 The entire series of articles can be found in Juan Bautista Morales, *El gallo pitagórico* (Mexico, 1845). The possibility that he may have authored *Consideraciones . . .* is also suggested by Vicente Fuentes Díaz in his *Gómez Farías: padre de la reforma* (Mexico, 1948), 213n.

12 The author's breakdown of Mexico's population differs slightly from later estimates made by students of Mexican society. C. E. Marshall has estimated that in 1803 the population of New Spain was 41% Indian, 19½% white, and 39% mestizo; and that in subsequent decades the proportion of pure Indians gradually decreased; see his "The Birth of the Mestizo in New Spain," *Hispanic American Historical Review*, XIX (May, 1939), 162-84. Eyler A. Simpson estimates the mix to have been 1/10 white, 6/10 mestizo, and 3/10 Indian at the time of independence; for this see his *The Ejido: Mexico's Way Out* (Chapel Hill, 1937), 18n. The difficulty in determining exact figures is due in part to the complex pattern of intermarriage and mutual acculturation that had been taking place in Mexico for a period of more than three centuries, and it has been suggested that by the time of independence the distinction between the different groupings was not so much racial or cultural as economic and social.

13 In the following discussion the author focuses sharply upon the distinctive position of the Indian population in Mexico, and in this view he is supported by such studies as Nathan Whetten's *Rural Mexico* (Chicago, 1948); and José E. Iturriaga's *La estructura social y cultural de México* (Mexico, 1951). It has also been argued, however, that acculturation and intermarriage were much more widespread than the author suggests, and that even by the period in question it was no longer possible to speak confidently of a purely Indian segment of Mexican society; for this view see Woodrow Borah, "Race and Class in Mexico," *Pacific Historical Review*, XXIII (November, 1954), 331-42.

14 Miguel Lerdo de Tejada found the amount of gold and silver legally exported from Mexico during the period 1825-1851 to average 9,120,233 pesos a year, but noted that there was also a significant amount of the metals exported illegally to escape export taxes. Lerdo de Tejada concluded that four-fifths of Mexico's exports during this period consisted of gold and silver, and the bulk of this was in the form of silver. See Miguel Lerdo de Tejada, *Comercio exteriór de México* (Mexico, 1967), 59-63.

15 Import duties of twenty five per cent *ad valorem* were established by a tariff act in 1842, and these were raised to thirty per cent in September, 1843. These were somewhat lower than the duties established by previous tariff acts, but were accompanied by a long list of import prohibitions that contributed to increased smuggling operations. See *ibid.*, 39-44.

16 While Church holdings in Mexico were considerable during this period their exact extent has been difficult to determine. Lucas Alamán, the conservative diplomat-historian, stated that the Church owned half the real estate in Mexico at the time of independence, while the liberal writer José María Luis Mora estimated the Church's total invested capital to be 149,131,460 pesos. Both these estimates have been attacked by Michael P. Costeloe for being too high; see his *Church Wealth in Mexico: A Study of the "Juzgado de Capellanías" in the Archbishopric of Mexico,* 1800-1856 (Cambridge, 1967), 86-87.

17 As the narrative indicates, one type of Church investment involved direct ownership of estates either willed to the Church or acquired through purchase, and occupied by tenants. In addition, however, the Church held mortgage on a considerable amount of income property. This usually came about when parishoners donated money to the Church in support of a specific activity, and the funds would be placed in medium or long term loans in order to produce a regular income for the desired activity. For a more extended discussion of this see *ibid., passim.*

18 The *Banco de Avío* was a government lending institution created in 1830 to promote the establishment of domestic industry, particularly in cotton textiles. Funds were provided for the bank from part of the revenues obtained through a tariff on crude cotton cloth. The bank operated with limited success for some years, and was abolished in 1842. Although the bank was the creation of the conservative spokesman Lucas Alamán it received support from some liberal quarters, including the *moderado* newspaper *El siglo diez y nueve.*

19 The prohibition was established in 1838.

20 The *Plan de Tacubaya* was a program for the reorganization of the Mexican government issued by Antonio López de Santa Anna, Gabriel Valencia, and Mariano Paredes y Arrillaga in September, 1841, as part of a revolutionary movement which overthrew the administration of Anastasio Bustamante. Under the terms of the *Plan de Tacubaya* Santa Anna became Provisional President of Mexico on October 9, 1841, and stayed in power until December, 1844. One of the controversial acts of his administration occurred in December, 1842, when he engineered the dissolution of the Constitutional Congress created by the *Plan de Tacubaya,* seemingly because it was on the verge of adopting a federalist constitution. Instead, an "Assembly of Notables" was appointed which drafted a centralist constitution called the *Bases Organicos,* which was promulgated on June 12, 1843. See José Fuente Mares, *Santa Anna: aurora y ocaso de un comediante* (Mexico, 1959), 174-76.

21 Led by the textile industry, manufacturing interests supported Santa Anna's rise to power in 1841, largely because of the belief that the loosened trade policies of the Bustamante government were responsible for the depressed state of domestic manufacturing. Santa Anna responded by increasing the prohibitions on imports in the trade acts of 1842 and 1843, as well as with the constitutional protection mentioned in the narrative above. See Robert A. Potash, *El Banco de Avío de México: El fomento de la industria,* 1821-1846 (Mexico, 1959), 200-06.

22 In the textile industry, at least, the rush appears to have begun as early as 1840, for production increased dramatically in that year over former levels. It sagged badly in 1842, and then recovered under the protection of the new trade acts. By 1845 production of cotton textiles was three times that of 1841, and roughly seven times that of 1840. See *ibid.,* 238-39.

23 At least two notable exceptions must be made to this generalization, both involving administrations directed by the *puro* leader Valentín Gómez Farías. From April, 1833 to April, 1834 he was in control of the government because of his position as Vice President, for Santa Anna, who was President, took a leave of absence. During this period Gómez Farías inaugurated a program to reform Mexican society. He ended the legal enforcement of the collection of tithes, secularized the California missions, and broke the Church monopoly over public education, all as part of a plan to reduce the influence of the Church in Mexican society. He was removed from office through a revolutionary movement in which Santa Anna himself took part, but returned to power in December, 1846, again as Santa Anna's Vice President. In the following months he attempted to seize Church *mortmain* properties in order to help finance the war against the United States, which led to another revolutionary movement aimed at his removal from office. Santa Anna responded to the revolt by persuading Congress to abolish the office of Vice President, and named the more conservative Pedro Anaya to rule as "Substitute President" while he continued in command of the army. See Vicente Fuentes Díaz, *Gómez Farías: padre de la reforma* (Mexico, 1948), 95-133, 205-27.

24 For a similar assessment of the policies adopted by the occupation forces see José María Roa Bárcena, *Recuerdos de la invasión norteamericana,* 1846-1848, *por un joven de entonces* (Mexico, 1947), II, 76-78, 100-01, 140-43; III, 146-50. Roa Bárcena also calls attention to the frequency of individual atrocities committed against Mexican civilians by members of the occupation army, however, particularly on the part of volunteer troops; see *ibid.,* II, 97-100.

25 Roa Bárcena also notes, however, that demoralization among both National Guard and regulars in the Veracruz garrison was widespread, and that on the day before the capitulation a majority among the National Guard favored evacuation of the city. Bitter accusations were exchanged between the commanders of the Veracruz garrison and General Santa Anna over responsibility for the surrender. General José Landero, Commandant of the Veracruz garrison, charged that his forces had been abandoned by the national government, and that in the absence of reinforcements, ammunition, or supplies from the interior his situation soon became hopeless. Santa Anna responded by imprisoning Landero, as well as General Juan Morales, military commander of the state of Veracruz, and General José Durán, who commanded the fortress of San Juan de Ulúa. See *ibid.,* II, 268-325.

26 The purpose of a chaplaincy was usually to provide for the saying of a certain number of masses each year for the soul of the chaplain's sponsor, or benefactor. The standard procedure was for the benefactor to arrange for the establishment of a chaplaincy in his will, and the sum he designated would be invested by an office of the Church (the *Juzgado*) to generate a permanent source of income. Whoever was designated to receive this income (the *capellán*) was then responsible to see that the masses stipulated in the will were said each year. Older chaplaincies tended to be underfinanced in the 1840's, as they had been established when living costs were lower. Most chaplaincies were capitalized at between 2000 and 6000 pesos, however, and were administered to provide an income of five per cent of the base figure. See Costeloe, *Church Wealth in Mexico,* 46-62.

27 In December, 1845, Mariano Paredes y Arrillaga headed a revolutionary movement that overthrew the government of José Joaquín Herrera. Paredes then served as "Interim President" from January to August, 1846, and attempted to lay the groundwork for the establishment of a monarchial form of government in Mexico. Frustrated in this design, he was overthrown by a revolution put together by *puros* and *santanistas* early in August.

28 The action referred to was called the revolt of *los polkos.* See also note 23.

29 There were five major political groupings in Mexico in the 1840's. Conservatives were divided into three camps: *santanistas,* monarchists, and *centralistas,* while liberals were categorized as *moderados* or *puros.* The conservatives were united in their desire for a centralized form of government, and in their desire of privileged positions for the Church, the military, and the dominant economic classes in Mexico. They differed, however, in their approach to the governing process. *Centralistas* favored a parliamentary form of government, while monarchists hoped to draw upon European royalty to establish a monarchy in Mexico. *Santanistas,* on the other hand, favored an authoritarian rule by Antonio López de Santa Anna. For a discussion of the *puro* and *moderado* divisions see note 3.

30 The reference is to Miguel Bataller, a Spanish magistrate who served in New Spain during the final years of colonial rule. A man of considerable abilities, he was offered political appointment in the government of Mexico when independence had been won, but returned to Spain instead.

31 Juan Martínez de Ripalda was a seventeenth century Jesuit theologian who taught at Salamanca and the Imperial College at Madrid.

32 The reference is to Lorenzo de Zavala, a liberal writer and statesman from Yucatán. In addition to leading an active political career, Zavala published a number of essays on Mexican society and political life prior to his death in 1836. He spent the final years of his life as a colonizer in Texas, and played an active role in the Texan revolution. At the time of his death he was Vice President of the Republic of Texas.

33 "Middle knowledge" is part of a system of theological thought known as Molinism, which was formulated by the Spanish Jesuit and theologian Luis de Molina in the latter part of the sixteenth century. The concept refers to God's prior knowledge of what the future acts of man would be in given circumstances if He chose to intervene in earthly affairs.

34 "Scotus" probably refers to the thirteenth century English theologian John Duns Scotus, and "Belarmino" to Robert Belarmino, an Italian Cardinal and theologian of the sixteenth and seventeenth centuries. "Mother Agreda," or Mary of Agreda, was a seventeenth century abbess of the Poor Clare monastary near Agreda, Spain, who authored a controversial biography of the Virgin Mary, as revealed to her in a vision.

35 Miguel de Grua Talamanca, the Marqués de Branciforte, served as Viceroy of New Spain from 1795 to 1798, and José de Iturrigaray held the same position from 1803 to 1808. Both men have frequently been criticized for using their positions for personal gain. See, for instance, Justo Sierra, *The Political Evolution of the Mexican People,* translated by Charles Ramsdell (Austin, 1969), 140-41, and Lillian Estelle Fisher, *The Background of the Revolution for Mexican Independence* (Boston, 1934), 309-11. For a defense of Branciforte, however, see David Bushnell, "El Marqués de Branciforte," *Historia Mexicana,* II (enero-mayo, 1953), 390-400.

36 Iturrigaray was forcibly deposed on September 15, 1808, by a pro-Spanish group in New Spain that suspected the Viceroy of planning the independence of Mexico with himself as ruler. Juan Ruiz de Apodaca, who served as the next to last Viceroy of New Spain during the years 1816-1821, abdicated on July 6, 1821 under pressure from his military commanders for allegedly mishandling military campaigns against Mexican forces fighting for independence. For a defense of Apodaca, however, see Francisco de Paula de Arrangoiz, *México desde* 1808 *hasta* 1867 (Mexico, 1968), 284-85.

37 The "refugee" government referred to was formed in the city of Querétaro following Scott's seizure of Mexico City on September 17, 1847. The provisional government was dominated by *moderados,* and under the leadership of Pedro Anaya and Manuel de la Peña y Peña it carried through the negotiations with Nicholas Trist that led to the Treaty of Guadalupe Hidalgo.